Tender Philosophia

Poems

by Didi Aphra & Jonna Leine

Cover design & illustration by Luisa Galstyan
Illustration by Didi Aphra
Edited by Evelyn Diamant
Edited by Vera Strobel

1st Edition 2024

ISBN 979-8-3348-7488-6 (paperback)

Printed in the United States of America

Published by Didi Aphra & Jonna Leine

For
J, whom the moon slipped between the shelves for me. And to
the dreamers who have been yearning all their lives.

Didi

For
my angel dog, whose orbit was my home. And to the misfits
who are still looking for the magic. It exists, be brave.

Jonna

TABLE OF CONTENTS

Jonna Leine

Acknowledgments

I would like to thank Jonna Leine for plucking my discarded daydream up from somewhere in the cosmos and breathing life into it again with your added flair, for without you it may well have been many years before I even dared to publish a book. We actually did it, you and I. You are the bright, beautiful soul I have always wanted to befriend. Thank you for showing up in my life.

Thank you to Evelyn Diamant and Vera Strobel for your generosity, support, and above all, honesty while editing our work. I am beyond grateful.

The *Percy Jackson and the Olympians* series, for igniting my love for Greek mythology when I was eleven. Sallie Lundh, for opening my eyes to the annual month-long poetry challenge that is Escapril, through which I started to shape my craft. And also for writing us a gorgeous review—better than either of us could have ever dreamed of. Savannah Brown, whose Escapril prompts have helped us through the last four years. Anna Harmon, for her support and incredible word wizardry that is our blurb.

Thank you to my parents for their support, even though the most I can utter about my poetry is a few vague words (the best a poet can do).

To the editors at the Dionysian Public Library: Ju Collins, Fritz Dries, and v.f. thompson. Thank you for accepting my poem, *Fallen Fruit,* and giving it a first home in *Propagate: Fruits from the Garden* in June 2024.

Thank you to my Elowen kitty, who sprung up in the woods one day and followed me home a week later. "You came back for me," you said. It was the most special meow I had ever heard. You showed me that the magick I believed in as a child exists.

And, undoubtedly, thank you to J, whose presence in my life is a safe harbor in a world of chaos. The understanding you have given me came sooner than I ever thought it would. You have seen *Tender Philosophia* grow up since its inception and have seen me grow with it and with you. Thank you for listening to all my ramblings and believing in me. Where would we be now if I had never written, if you had never written? You called out from that place our souls are made of and I answered. Or was it the other way around?

Didi

I would like to thank Didi Aphra for being the friend I always dreamed of. For the love and care and eternal inspiration. Without you, I'd be a lonely speck of dust on the cosmic canvas of existence.

Thank you, Evelyn Diamant and Vera Strobel, for the guiding light you gave us while editing this book. Thank you, Sallie Lundh, for your beautiful advice and even more stunning review. Thank you, Anna Harmon, for the gorgeous blurb. Thank you, Savannah Brown, for hosting Escapril which helped us to keep writing. Thank you, Orion Carloto, whose comment section was where Didi and I first met on social media. See, something beautiful can come out of social media when you treat it with the same light you carry within.

This collection covers many years of our short lives. A lot has changed. A lot has been sustained.

Thank you to my mom who taught me to be resilient. Thank you to my angel dog who was always the first audience for my poetry. Thank you to those who stayed. Thank you to those who left, life is lighter now. Thank you to the one who accedes to my reveries. Thank you to the one who mentored me with acceptance and care. Sorrowful nights, iridescent mornings, which is life. Which is poetry.

What is done with love, is done well. Look at us now Didi. Our intensity, hyperboles, the fairy dreams, hypotheses… The moon had its siren song–this is ours.

Jonna

Didi Aphra

Because I Do

But what about all the things we never said to
each other? The longing glances we shared in
public places, kept most private in our hearts?
Red velvet curtains drape softly over
mahogany wood, their collected dust telling
the eons gone by. *Eons.* Back to the
beginning of time. Did your tadpole heart
beat for me then? In the laurel woodlands of
evolution, did your primal body yearn for me?
Do you search for me now, in each rose garden
you pass? Each berry you eat? Do you devour
the sweet juices of blackberries, let the fruit
burst in your mouth and savor the taste?

I ask you because I do.

Abyssopelagic

Sing me your morning song with the pensive tune
that makes the wind stir with trepid violence
of its own desire, seizing sails spellbound
that they may swelt slowly into the earth's wide
mouth, no more standing hoplite, hussar, dragoon

Sing me your evening song so tonight that I might
see the devotion that you hold for me when in
the night's final hour, the most abyssal ardors
within me rush forth, requiting archaic hymns
unsung for too long even I have forgotten,
no more waiting miserere, mercurial, divine

Throwaways

This is as good a place as any, thought God
when he plucked us from the heavy branches and plopped
us in the deep blue sea.
        And so down we fell.
Little earthling sprouts making our way through the world
shedding too many tears on our cotton pillows and
wanting for heart-shaped everythings.
        Spilled mulled wine all
over the place when you first confessed your love
on my bed. I'd closed up all the drapes, made it look like
a place of worship. It's laughable now, how easily
we fell, what a mess we made after.
        We'd been too careful
our whole lives, too good to continue on. He had nothing
to do with it. Not when he tossed us aside just like
that. Underwater undeservers only now getting air.
        And it comes in gasps.

They Forget How Softly Eros Walked

West wind moves daylilies wild at my feet as
you touch my face, softer than the pierced
heart of Eros as he gazed at Psyche in her
sleep. They did not love so tenderly for us to
fall prey to the judgment of
minds that never once bathed in the
iridescent waterfalls at the center of the
cosmos. Looked onward at the thousand
blazing suns, kissed each other 'til breathing
was merely a pastime—*hold my hand*, I say,
more delicately than dandelion seeds wandering
free in the summer air.

Didi Aphra & Jonna Leine

Love on Hands and Knees

What does artificial intelligence know
about love? It could never know the
divine sweetness with which you make me want.
So what if it advances humanity, so what?
It could never know that it's enough
to be like bugs in the dirt. Primal yearning
and all that. It could get on its
(artificial) hands and (hypothetical) knees
and howl at the moon, sure. But
what good would that do? It would
interpret that command as a zoanthropic
fantasy or throw in something about Allen
Ginsberg, maybe. But it would never know the love
that exists between each tangerine peel and
each time you tell me about your day.

Nowhere

I dream without moving my feet. In these walls, I see
temples and the waterfall retreat. Like how I kiss your temples
when your head hurts from your hidden hurt.

I crawl inside you and my head gets dizzy from all
your wonders. Your Alexandrian stories tucked away,
a hidden library of first editions.
I travel through the Louvre of your sorrow, see the
bearded man encircled by blue.

I hold you, I hold you.

On the train ride through Europe—the place you noticed
my soul resides. I am from nowhere.

Godly Want

What if I swallowed the moon? Would my belly
swell up and glow—pregnant, radiant, goddess-like?
And the gods, would they envy my celestial child?
Would they, too, swallow it after it was born—
castrate my pride?

Oceanids

Let us run away to the other realm where words are spoken in
liquid tongues and we laugh ourselves into honeyed bubbles
as the Cruel World burns in a cauldron in the castle
atop the hill

Let us be caressed awake by the morning mist,
hold wildness in our stomachs as we morph into sanguine
streams and again into the shapes of each other's most
delirious dreams

Inside Me Sits A Three-Headed Dog

Let me kiss the neurons in your brain that ache,
the tendons of your bones that shake,
the sinews of your flesh that break.
My mind exists in the nether realm
but my body craves the corporeal.
I want to consume you the way Cerberus
eats raw flesh, but tenderly
in the way lovers do.

If Cupid meant to strike us both, then
let us combust into the stardust we were made of.
Be mine! My phantasmagoric yearning exclaims.
Let my body enamor you until your blood thickens,
flesh dying to make room for me. *Come to me,
come, my darling. Come!* We'll ascend through
Cancer back into the spilt milk of Hera,
where our souls once lay.

Some Venerean melancholia incited this,
or so the Renaissance scholars say. Eros
crafted me from clay, it is he who made me
the *daemon magnus*. They pray for
nothing. *Don't pray, don't pray.* All are lost
to me. But still, lying beneath me, your magic
brings me to rapture. No rotations of the
iliac crest may satiate such famine. I shiver with
unbridled want, as I do day after day.

If Not, Winter

As the yolk of the midnight sun begins to dive back down the
horizon, beaded eyes of the stag stare back, taunting.
Persephone! Screams Demeter,
kicking up granite on the trail.
Wind whispers rumors of the fleshly scarlet seeds that had
traveled down Persephone's throat.
Her eyes go glassy as she swallows, spying star seeds.
When will you return to me, dearest daughter?
Have I lost you forever?
The Goddess strips the earth bare in mourning
as Persephone's caged heart unravels in the shadow realm.
Each honest confession from the dark God closes in on her
moat, the black-watered river.

To The Unseen One

i. that which you whispered to me in the stairwell made my
ears turn red with need. i did not know i had it in me. rather, i
did, but it was not for shame. in fact of shame, i am emptied. it
is the bittersweet other that burns within.

ii. i am only sorry i could not follow you into the depths to
carve out the soft flesh of your sadness and feed it to myself.

iii. with you i feel the loosening of the limbs, or is it the soul?
perhaps it's the tightening, screwing, cinching of it that undoes
me all over again.

Moonbathing

At the peak of a midsummer's night, cherry trees drink in
the moonlight, fresh and unhurried, rouge skin beaming
with wonder.

The moon tells me things no one else has, secrets immortalized
through her constance. Will you let me drink you in like the
moonlight? Welcome you in like god on the terrace of
my soul?

Sweet Briar

I can do it, you know she says in the soft candlelight.
              I know, I say.

Our nights had been full of kisses too chaste to call sacred.
It took the halving of a pomegranate—
              seeing what I could do to blushing flesh
                        —for us to bend over to worship.

She, the goddess, me on my knees at the altar, praying.
Only we were equals, devouring fruits
              always ready for the harvest—
                        —coloring in the lines
                                  softly with our tongues.

My body is made of longing. I keep it alive to devour the
divine. The eglantine vines shoot out from your breasts,
entangling my body closer to yours until our hips, thighs,
              shoulder blades are outlined by the earth—

—peach-pink petals attached, stigmas latching,
and sepals twining around my ankles. The greenery
of our wanting devotes itself to a shrine, reciting
              panegyrics with each eventide.

Fallen Fruit

And today we fell with strawberried tongues,
a half blush deep inside our bellies
from soft-bodied fruit
So close to that delectable feeling—
what was it? Happiness?
How amorous the plants are outside
those French windows, bees making love
which you imitated with your thumb
on curved flesh close, so close to the center
I could hear soft hymns from the Muses
echoing in my ear, I could feel the droplets
of dew fall from sighing wildflowers

Maybe My Lover Is My Gift From God

Have I gone insane? Sometimes I find myself wondering if
You are simply a figment of my imagination. *Is he real?*
Are you real? How are you real? You came to me in a dream
And now your words imbue my nocturnal mind. *How is it so?*
Am I insane? Darling, tell me, tell me!

What about you, God? What are your wishes? Your dreams?
If I can't find you in the crocuses blooming in the dead of
winter, in the fallen pomegranates threatening to split the forest
floor to descend to the Underworld, how do I live? Are your
wishes like falling stars? Dried roses? Are your dreams in the
anguish of Orpheus's eyes after he turns around?

Sometimes I think I find you in the whispered words in
between lines of poetry, in the gentle morning light, the weeds
sprouting in the garden after a heavy rain. Maybe you live in
between the stained sheets of lovers, open-mouthed kisses on
navels, or that frenzied moment of unspeakable pleasure.

Dying Embers

Who are they to judge the things we have done,
the cries of ghosts only we can hear?
Let's light up the forest with our lovely hurt.

Squirrels peek from their hide and moss breathes life
into the dead undergrowth. Don't they know how
the sweetness of the fallen apple colors the soul?
How the wolf repents?

Lying here on the cold, dark earth,
who knew she could love us so well?
Ashes, ashes. Oh, to be licked by the passionate blaze!
It is true what they say, the burnt child
loves the flame.

Blueberry

Tell me where your pain is. Hop on the
carousel going nowhere, going everywhere.
Isn't that what they tell us? What goes around
goes nowhere? What of pi then? I watch your
blueberry eyes stare into my soul, *ad infinitum.*
Thump, thump, goes your heart. Your story
paints the whole room blue. It's through the
harbor of your words that I learned
the color blue could be so warm.

1:23 a.m.

It was just an illusion. The way black ooze falls from
the sky and my thoughts break the lock in my mind at 1:23 am.
A sped-up silent film of a space walk
playground made of red blood cells in vaginal walls and other,
indescribable horrors.
The way the figure stands at the edge of the bed
and chains my ankle to the post—not to have fun but to break
me from the inside.

The darkened street has a conscience. The paintings,
too, have morals. Unable to look away, the mahogany drapes
on my four-poster bed wrap themselves around the figure's
neck, rendering him a fragile, suffering thing.

And I shrink back into myself, curled in the covers on a
gentle October night. Nothing's wrong, it's not real—
not the distant howls of famished wolves, not
the yellow fog rubbing its breasts against window panes, not
the faces frozen mid-scream in tree trunks.

Come sunrise the world will be soft again.
Days measured out in coffee scoops, a million grinning beans
shipped from sunny lands.
I try to drink in the sunshine—the warmth
of the golden light—to fill that spot
inside me with a vital brightness so never again would I
have to see those horrors.

Forget Me Not

The Garden of Eden
was where we met. I was picking daffodils and
           there you were. At once I found myself bitten with
passion, innocence slithering away into the daisy shrubs.

I wanted to coil into myself,
round and round, my body pulled taut ready to
           snap. To feel you curled behind me tighter, 'til death
gave in and lilacs sprung from our flatlands, an insignia of
remembrance and desire.

Kiss me into the earth's core,
I wanted to feel the heat, but my body wasn't ready for it any
           more than you were mine. Not yet, at least. What is
falling in love if not some form of delayed gratification,
especially with you.

The way you tease,
it makes death seem heavenly. Every touch, every kiss of yours
           is not without a motif. Is that why you, before
professing your love, brought me to the bush seasoned with
roses? And before our first kiss, we just so happened upon the
mallow flowers?

And when you thought you
were about to draw your last breath, you whispered that you
           would meet me in the meadow and told me to dream of
laying with you in a field of forget-me-nots.

As if I could ever forget you.

Crystalline Dream

I envy the black satin that slips over her skin,
Nightstand lavender that gets to watch her sleep
How bright into the future she sees
Oh, but how easily into the dreamscape she slips
I can only wonder
Must I bruise my body inside her amethyst geode
If only to follow her into wonderland?
See the ripples in her turquoise waters?
I wish to be the sunlight that kisses her cheeks
on Sunday mornings
I wish to be the shower water that glides down her back
I wish to exist in the sea of halved fig seeds
she brings to her lips

Vena Amoris

Pillow soft, I hold your gaze
More tender still are your wrists,
the inside of your wrists
I bring my lips to the blues of your veins,
kiss the violet tendrils
that keep you alive,
the hands you use to feel me,
fingers I make love to
What I clutch at night as I fall asleep

Daughter of Libra

It's getting dark and I just might
crawl back
home. It's getting dark and
I just might
slip into the
earth, the dirt. Watch the rain fall onto me and
wash away my worries.
The archway of creeping jasmine
flaunts its scent with
quiet judgment,
watching me water myself like a
plant because I'm
the only one who will not leave me.
I will not leave I will not leave
I will not
throw myself off a moving ship
in the sea of
lost souls
because my scales are ever-balanced.
I bleed only for myself,
retreating into maternal darkness
under many-mooned Jupiter.

Moments Before Eclipse

On the dark side of the sun, we hang
our heads for the unspoken truths.
Long for a taste of we know not what.
Broken souls buried in the dirt, a
shattered heart served on a silver platter.
A true love's kiss.

> On the bright side of the moon, we
> scream that joy is coming, she writhes
> on ocean waves. Onlookers suspect
> she's a passenger of air. But they don't know
> the sheer terror of unquenchable want. They
> don't know how the ocean was once a
> nymph in love. They don't know
> how she reaches for the moon.

Being Lilith's Daughter

Please, Mother, I am trying to be good.
      I
killed one last night with   my desire.
   NOT GOOD ENOUGH!
she thunders, shredding my pride to pieces.
But how am I to be my best without your love?
      You told me   that
we are to be lethal to defend ourselves, the better to
match the   monstrous fibers
  mens' hearts are made of.
      Your words are drops of wolfsbane *(aconitum)* I
swallow   every day. Tomorrow I shall
use the stench of the corpse flower *(amorphophallus titanum)*
in assisting my next one's meeting with Charon. A
smile, malefic.
      How fitting that they shall meet the face of Death with
one of their own.

Sapiosexual

The way you spoke lit a fire on the back of my neck
and the touch of your eyes, too, left me a wreck
But in them, I saw the weariness of Atlas holding up the sky
Through your words, I felt the hands of our souls
entwine and sigh

Lay your head on my lap, I said, soon after we first met
It felt so right, like slipping into bed at the end of the day,
I couldn't help but feel it was the stirrings of kismet
So just for a moment, lay your head down and
let me carry the weight of your world

Children of Gaia

I watched you bring the peach pit to your lips. Flickers of
last night played in the soft curves of your gentle smirk.

I halve my peach and watch it spread open on the
cutting board. A drop of juice trickles silently down your chin.
I lick it off.

Tell me your secrets, I ask of the fruit, ever-present Mother
Earth. I raise the plump peach to my lips.

Didi Aphra & Jonna Leine

One for the Witch in the Woods

This is the spot where you and I meet
But where do you begin and where do I end?

Your knees—the tops of Corinthian columns
hold up our very own temple

How else is love meant to be taken?

How do I know what is mine when I feel
you in the taste of every comma?

I am a galaxy of kisses I haven't given
Espy my glimmer in the wych elm groves,

lurking in the clandestine corners where cloves
chant their very own spell

Actaea Pachypoda

Sly October mist rises at the crack of dawn,
beckoning their sisters to creep
Creep to the skies, creep over our eyes
A slurry of fog slinks its tail over my neck
and down my waist, and lower still

It takes me on a ride inside the
strangest dream
The rest of them gather near,
watching mesmerized
At the outline of my body, the lashes
round my all-seeing eyes

Sappho and Erinna

In the velvet nights, my tornado curls drape your
immaculate cheeks. Bathed under the dreamy moon,
Euphoria comes to fly us away,

imprisoned by voluptuousness and chained in
violent pleasures. Vivacious death upon your hands—
my roses stripped of their thorns, tracing the stars on
your ivory skin.

Forlorn

The love bequeathed to me
By her   were

But droplets of morning dew
I sit   here

Forlorn

Phantasy of a Prey

I was an   ingenue,
               doe-eyed beauty

He was   a buck
     at the season of mating

I was a snake
     at the height of danger

Open wide,   he said
              so I did
     and I swallowed him
   whole

My long body
     stretched to his shape

Hanging Up My Wings To Dry

    I was consumed by the hunger of my skin.
Melted into a cocoon, my tired wings
        laid out to rest.

    In the battle of wire and wool, I chose the latter
to soothe my aching soul,
        touch-starved, capitulated.

Writer's Manifesto

May I write about my tender self, dying to be loved. May I
write about the complex aching my heart has known since
birth. A longing for more, more than this. But at the same time
so much less. All I need are singing birds and apples cherry red
and an evergreen embrace from the forest to be reborn again.
I died this winter but I am alive as ever.

Wisteria

It is what our love lives on—intricate trails of
knowledge traveling at the speed of light (more like
the speed of a snail, to be honest). We pour our love
into a cauldron of playlists. A teasing note of the violin—
Tchaikovsky.

A hiss and violet smoke weans up, villain-like, as tree roots
stretch underground. Do you smell that rawness in my
sap? Pungent in fertile dirt.

My branches wax to the west, sprouting flowers like jewels on
a sacred tree. Wisteria perhaps—
weeping downwards in lonesome glory.

My tendons reach in search of you
slowly, achingly, in the forbidding dark.

Descendants of the Sea

It was almost like we were opposites—we were
masculine, feminine, one and the same.
Beings on earth at once tasting the light and the dark.
Emanating the feminine through your ocean of words, the pearl
of your sensual kiss.

It is like we are gods, the beings who spawned from their
minds, their swollen egos. We are their descendants,
spawns, siblings, distant cousins.
When you close your eyes you can see inside me
and I in you.

Would that you were an oyster, I would see the world
in your shining, iridescent luster. I'd wrap my lips
around each layer of nacre, greedy
for more until the waves birth us from our mortal bodies.

Drinking Poetry

Nothing beats the contemplation of the phrase
"starving hysterical naked" like it did when I was first hit by
the genius of Howl, full force freight car, ravenously drinking
poetry gold, the planted seed to which turned a rose proud and
grandiose to which formed a secret garden, fertilized by love,
      true naked only

when the day is in recess we lay in bed and undress,
soul bare intellect, heart-wrung poems freshly poured like
coffee black how you need it in the mornings, the essence of
the bean from the sweet red berries from the sun-loving trees,
how you need the essence of my soul, shiny pink stream in the
valley opposite of black goo
      river Styx, how the fruit juice ripens

when the earth tilts towards the sun again, drawing
upon ichor warmth to replenish branches left bare naked in the
forest on the streets to the laughing chlorophyll children sat on
window sills to foyers to patios to balconies,
      love their only fertilizer

when the soft flesh of your body screams to be held,
the sleeves of my empathy will hold you close, you cling on
like a bee to an open flower
in the height of summer sipping on nectar, the honey
      I make for you

Stardust

Do you know what we are made of?
stars burst behind my eyes at the height of pleasure
I saw where we came from, you and I
love served in sweet moans
They said we were fated from the moment of birth
two hearts thumping out of their cages
Like on lazy Sunday mornings when two pieces
of butter melt back into each other on the pan
touches, tantalizing
A shovel of dirt back into the earth
heavy sighs in between kisses
The tails of two cats curled into a heart
a teasing kiss to the back of the ear
The way tea sighs into a cup at the first pour
more, please

Kraneia

When I think of you, crimson roses bloom
from the blood of my beating heart and
vines of ivy spring from my hair.
I cannot help but let the
myrtle and coriander flowers drape
on my body, the scent of
early morning love to fall undisguised.

Cruel Worship

Where the lava boils, fury releases inside me—
bulbous fibers that gently caress swimming spheres.
Behold!
The sacred butterfly is raging again
Strawberry stream, detestable scream,
heart-stopping dreams.
I was leaning off kilter when it all began—
as a sunflower slants when teased by the sun
that every morn rises. Now noontide befalls
and all is returned to the center.
My veins are colored in crimson supplied by you,
my holy enchantress.
What say you? Do I pass?
Does my erubescent veil warm your heart enough?
Would that you were a leopard I would
charm you with my grace only for you to be pierced,
torn apart by these canines sharp.
Is that sweet enough, cruel enough, my demonic mother?
My eyes shed blood in worship of you

Potion

      With these hands I reached
inside myself
and found   ink in deep burgundy.
It stained my hands, kept spilling,

                     and spilling

      all over my garden and my bed.
Over my eyes and my head

        I spill love unto myself

      Had this elixir been brewing
all these years? Left fermenting to such
     vermilion richness?

        Did I grow it myself from the seeds
of betrayal?

Aphrodite's Temple

The shadow of your love casts us against midnight-hour blues. Lace against thighs and the magic of my fingerprints on your chest. Molecular love in each particle of your lips. Did you know I feel you in my dreams? We were walking on the stone steps of the juniper temple, where the waterfall whispered sweet nothings in our ears. An ambient light glowed from between two trees and I asked you to take a silhouette picture of me standing naked before the light. Each time we stopped on the sacred tracks, your lips would seek my neck, eager kisses down the curve, the nape, my shoulders, a love path down my back.

Frisson

I can give you life as Isis did Osiris, but the
power you give me when you fall apart in my hands
as the sun rises is a rebirth of its own kind

Daytime yearning. Heart sledging along each
tick of the clock. I hide among the bookshelves in search
of your scent still lingering between the vellum.

In the fading hours of the day,
I come undone at the foot of your throne.

Homesick

It is unspeakable—the spot where they tore off my wings
They bit them right off with their tiny little mouths
Now my
back aches all the time with their phantom weight
I miss the
taste of sweet ambrosia and the scent of nectar springs
and how
even after all the cornucopia gave you still only
had an appetite for me

Persephone's Repentance

Sweet seeds of death,
I am bound to you forever
Now I bathe in the onyx rain
Death garden in sweet rest
They fear me, for I am the last judgment
I left as the white flowers bloomed,
Came as the red fruits ripened beneath

Bacchanalia

Why, in the delirium of appetency, are we expected
to create? If it's an animal instinct, maybe I'm
not an animal. Did I miss some brainwashing class
where they drill into us that we must associate the
act of creation with love?

In the presence of desire, I only know how to want
you and nothing else. The essence of pleasure,
nothing beyond. I only know the brain static of
ecstasy, the toe curls, the moment when maybe we
are insane, touched by some Dionysian spirit.

June

It's June and my heart is finally free
Laying on the forest floor,
I crawl into your flaws and make it
my home, the way moss clings
to tree bark

How To Exist

i. To be so comfortable in your presence that I don't
bother to hide my cheeks, to let you kiss the
ruby blush of a ripe nectarine.

ii. Breathe in the trees of pleasure in The Garden.

iii. The reading of a good book bound with the same
engravings as the ones on my soul.

iv. The beauty of friendship. Simply
telling you about my day.

v. Letting the wolf inside me make friends with
the moon, letting her howl out her longing.

vi. Find the waves thrilling—riveting, even—
to ride when all it does is ask more than I can give.

I, Whose Soul You've Held In Your Hands

Maybe you are bound by the claws of lust,
but I fear that for me, it is more like gluttony.
And with it I carry no indignity, only the
unsatisfied thirst of Tantalus reaching for ripe
fruit. But you've been craving too, haven't you?
I see it in the unrestrained predilection with
which you gaze at me.

Lovers' Liaison

All day I feel your fingers etched into my skin,
leaving your mark. The language of love is in your
hands when you take me to the library and show me
the books that made you who you are.

All around us, books fall apart from the
crushing weight of our captivation, waxing disbelief at the
way we abandon ourselves in mere letters, the space
between the lines.

Perhaps Our Time Is Up

My love, perhaps
      our time
      is up.

      May we meet again when
rosy-fingered dawn sighs softly in pastel,
when her gentle light caresses swaying
lavender fields.

      May we rest in the nest of
homecoming, prepared for us by the fresh
exhale of the death.

      You told me once that we would
love each other for the rest of the time we
have on this planet.

      We have met in centuries past,
our souls know no other, who's to say
we shall not
meet again?

Little Red

You want me to eat more but it is I who,
time and time again, find you starving and
make you eat. Come into my kitchen hungry,
kiss my neck while I'm standing at the sink,
lay me down on the table. *(dinner)*
In the languid mornings when
the sanctity under the covers is incense of its
own kind, the woman in the painting sighs.

You say I should eat more but it is I who,
time and time again, find you aching and
make you eat. Find you riding on my sweet scent,
led by your wolf's nose. What's cooking on the
stove, sweetheart? *(a path of kisses up my nape)*
Mushrooms propagate themselves
in the pan, procreating upon death.
Utensils lay bare, waiting to be touched.

You tell me to eat more but it is I who,
time and time again, find you ravenous and
make you eat. Familiar hands on my hips, dress
riding up my thighs. A question on my lips
for what comes after. *(dessert, darling)*
Melodic notes weave through our
longing on display for the shelves, the legs
of the books spread wide in prurience.

Perfume Moon

What does the moon smell like? The rabbit asks me one night.
The softest embrace of December snowfall, I reply.
Love her from afar and still she bathes you in her light.
Gunpowder is what the astronauts say,
but I don't know, I've never been to the moon.
Maybe the poetry of her beauty makes her smell that way,
aiming shots at soft hearts, young and old at doom.
If love is a disease, who wouldn't want to fall prey?
For loving is all we poets know.

Love Finds Us With Our Backs To It

Dew drops fall golden off hydrangea blooms
in the blink of an eye just as love catches us when our backs
are turned with the swallowing of the belief that it
belongs in fairytales.

It finds us sleeping on our stomachs so as not
to see the demon in the dark—shows us that he is a gentleman,
stuck in a hopeless haunt because he hasn't seen
his dead wife in a hundred years.

And we convince ourselves that we are not
worthy of love, that it is for people who find delight in
endless soirées and single-use plates.

In the grip of darkness when your skin is burning
and heart aching, love finds you with gentle hands curved
around your never-perfect belly and holds you
with more tenderness than you've ever felt.

For Once, It Is I Who Laughs At The Fates

You, darling, are my wish under a full moon.
My north star, my anchor, my tether to this world.
Under the blue moon gone blurry in our line of sight,
I ride the undulating waves of your love,
our heads thrown back, laughing at the cruel, cruel fates.
What's Moirai to our love?
What's the thread of life to our love when I have seen us
laying together in the Fields of Elysium for eternity?

Jonna Leine

Lucid Dreaming

I start fires to bring light.
In the heated hues
two shadows exist.
My ghost frame draws close,
soft palm caressing yours.
In your dream, you feel entranced
as if your skin has just been kissed.

Meanwhile on Earth

i. Darkness can envelope
you in, so your bones
melt and trickle down
from a cosmic mailbox.

ii. You might miss the earth,
so your hands reach further
and further towards the
ground, until it swallows you.

iii. Expectation can become your
morning song, and from your
bed to your desk you carry
the atlas of your worry.

iv. You might lose a day or a lover
and owe your body to the grief
that demands your kneeling
and all of your blind devotion.

v. As you shape around your
sadness, you become a servant
of the dark, and all the while the
apple tree grows a bloom above
your head.

Identities

But who am I
if not oneself as another;
given name but no meaning.
An empty beat,
an arrow against the tension of one's lips.

You shot it like a title,
a beginning with no writer.
A folk tale passed between the two,
I am simply imagined when it comes to you.

Selene

The night is patient, a test of love.
"You lay eternally lonely now"
I whisper to my sleeping body.
The room is silent, the dream is too.
It is brave to shut the eyes
when a soul can slip out like this.

Corpse-like oblivion in its haven,
stark-white sheets wrinkled and
the pale moon casting a crescent
on the temple of your deckled skull.
How alone, how alone are you
in the quiet house, the quiet blue.

You dream not of love, but for
someone to remember, but just wait;
earth breeds violets, roses, the…
The meaningless hours of your temper.
Two limp wrists in their rumination,
you reach for the shape of Death.

Lovers knew you weep at night
in unconscious solitude and fear.
Whatever you tried to shield yourself from
well… the danger laid within.
Now as the frozen corpse you again
scream with your baby lungs.

Isn't it quiet?
Isn't it lonely?

But that's a stone you picked
and carried into the purple night.
You're my tenant, and I am yours.

I forgive you.

Promnesia

I am colors and movements
while watching your words
start to come into existence.
Puffy lips press syllables, moving
absentmindedly between teeth.
I know them already, *déjà-vu*.

I act surprised, hush the need
to tell you the precognition I got.
It happens often, recurring dreams,
the next minute, (h)our, lifetime.
You will hang on to the term,
roll one eye, judge with the other.

I hum silently, watch people appear
just like I knew they would, hear
the words I knew I would,
look at things occur, like omens,
I don't care–
Je l'ai déjà vu.

To my left,
Eve shivers in blue.
But turning my head
would cause
a butterfly effect.

Pirates Bonny and Read

Some people appear like sails on the sea.
Air shakes its head and hands and
like the curves of a heart on the doctor's screen,
the mast is drawn,
then the ship and finally, the name attached to her.

The ship is harbored, the crew
busy with their beers, manifold Junes
pass the salt stone-scented, sepia-colored
port of misfit dreamscapes.

You wait, patient Robin song, your hand
against the hull, looking for the ancient old
focal mark; transparent ink where the ocean
hugs the craft, a gauze of lost, remote years.

You sailed off once, a sacrament of summer fear,
the pearl stayed in her silver boudoir.
You'd send away the stars too, but you've known
no heaven before her; persistently her.

Where the darkness comes in pirating light,
an infantile sun begins anew. Ebbs and flows,
she again. The harbor, the land, the birds:
a seagull with fresh fish. Your steadfast sparrow-mind.

Your craft, her touch, her morning light,
the sunburnt shape of you.
In each harbor, each life,
her oceanlike, opalescent hue.

Two Athenas

You see, my earthly luster,
my latest sleep is still here,
tangled on each surface of this room:
globes of peonies, pink powder scent.

There's this sense of being broken–come,
push your new hands through me;
you wouldn't change a thing, only
stars in your palms, my antique trinkets.

The heart would   beat,
the brain would sing compulsive songs.
Fatal, my new shape must be:
you were born from my temple.

Now, you are all sweet and unfilled,
I, the sheer light.

Apollo and Daphne

Here runs the river of life,
followers with dry feet.
Daphne in galactic dress
dances to the drum of a heartbeat.

The air shivers lilac-scented,
the sun sparkles on water swirls.
Like first love blooms innocence
above the rich, supple red curls.

Metamorphosis through summer screams.
Predators search for their prey,
forcing freckled faces on riverbeds.
Past the laurel trees, flows the bourne opaque.

And We Begin Again

Damp forest, snowy cotton
piles already rotting.
Filthy feet had left prints
on snow, on me, paths annihilated.

I asked the wind if she knew me,
recognized me from a time before.
Back when I donned a different shape:
round, square, caterpillar, poof.

A waft of smoke engulfed me.

Holding an unformed figure,
creature of unsheltered glow.
It is not defined nor printed,
no apparent testimonies.

As if when we lock eyes, and I am
empty, except for this alienated call
to rest my inner self, where you once
called me to begin again.

Poof
and we begin again.

Didi Aphra & Jonna Leine

Light Flickers in Human Heads

Maybe Forever got lonely.
Promises married to our mouths.
Church aisle, candlelit, mourners,
destinies doomed on Verona balconies.

*Forever, you don't belong here,
light flickers in human heads.*

Come, silence the storm in creators.
Help them release the strings.
Let their feet get wet, bewildered.
Give rest to their overflowing visions.

Even now, after everything,
they stayed virgin-minded
and in their dreams

where they gently tried out realities,
a certain forever remained wanted.

Polluted Lust

There's a beehive in the air conditioning.
We lie on the floor, covered by carbon dioxide
freshly pressed through the bee bodies.
"You smell like honey."
Dust grows from the rug
creating unstable statues
as the glow from the kitchen
travels through them, yellow,
unnatural, bouncing bouncing
like my fingers on your skin.
"Do you even hear me?"
I part my lips vaguely
and show you:
on my watering tongue
lies a bee asleep.

Paradox

What if stars going through extinction
are only mirrors to human depression.
No, let me rephrase that.
What if human depression is caused by
stars demising, burning to death.
Everything you sense in this absurd world
is dust, and we are energy, but where
is the endless power supply feeding us?
Are we just energy sucked up in a black hole,
glowing in nothingness, as little creatures
eat our brain and make us see eternal dreams?
Dreams in which you are right now reading this,
are you really? Do you hear that unfamiliar
buzzing, or smell that milky way smoke?
What if when we fall asleep, we get lost
in a wormhole and our senses get mixed up.
You'll never know for sure; I'll never know.
Maybe nothing exists but the moon and the stars
and we are already extinct, incessantly traveling in time.

Now I Am Nervous

It is a rare Finnish gold rush,
when springs reflect a midsummer's dream.
She once spoke Shakespearean
and now I am nervous.
Terrestrial orbit, satellite traffic,
time makes us forget
only if we write over it.
But I stopped writing,
to remember.
Who could do more than hope,
when seasons vary and fortunes lie.
Now I am here, and I am nervous.
Heat is rare in the north.

Wishbone

As we break the wishbone
we raise our eyes to Orion.
Make a wish, you see further.

We stand on melting roads,
unable to name the constellations
that brought us here.

Yet this is where we meet.
No flesh, just bones,
scared of ourselves.

Let me draw flowers
in the sand, and name them
after the nicknames
I secretly gave you.

See, I know you can see it.
The dead stars can,
the broken bones in graves can.
I should shut up now
before the mirage
gets all too real.

Pastime

Shoot me to the sky and let the clouds
wear me out in events for misfortunates
where I sway to the rhythm of sangria and
I am befriended by Zeus and the rest of the gods.
Let me hold descent as a postcard
to wave it like a missionary in search of
gates to beyond the cloudy pool of thoughts.

Push me as hard as you can, push me away.
Make scary faces and phases like a moon
I see under your lashes and what if your eyes
are moons and they fall out for rolling them
too much, you see the world from the floor,
I am the color in them, I am the trash on
corridors sticking to your clammy skin.
I keep your eyes closed, feel the whirlpool.

Travel soundly on my back while we
lure the serpentine roads out of valleys.
We show them cities and hotels and motels
and my casket waiting in the dark, but it is
actually, just a bonfire for witches never burnt.
I am a moving vehicle, filled with sour blushings,
snow buntings, restless hauntings, and nests.
Nestle under my skin, shoot me to the sky.

Aldebaran

But my soul is not an organ
it is a small purple stone
in intergalactic connection
to whatever breathes
or is forlorn.

Delicate Decay

I heard once, poetry is the art of linkages,
how through writing you put two in one

(I am a subject
signifying a delicate decay)

and someone writing about *us*
may bring you so close
we become a metaphor.

Two skins merged
is a new language,
a new set of eyes
coloring what always, already was there.

In the act of becoming a poem
we are set free,
we represent more
than was ever really exchanged
between us.

I Knew You Before You Were Born, You Were The Very Last Thought I Had

I passed through the barley field,
where ladybugs crawled
and we once frolicked too.
Hot air swirled, lifting up sand,
veiling the old cart road's traces.
The sun's faint halo pierced through,
embracing me in golden fog,
leaving only my tear-stained imprint behind.
Across the yellow haze
memories blurred, mistaking me for someone
who can find joy within longing.
I can hardly find myself!
In the blinding amber blaze,
I dissolved into the feeble scene.
In the golden darkness, all of me
turned into yellow dust,
and all I asked of you was this:
Come, breathe me in,
shape me anew.

Peridot

Leaning towards what is now empty,
disorientating, dissolving peridot stars.
New souls say it's proper to forget,
while braiding hair becomes a ritual
in wisteria-covered planetariums.

Meteorite lockets on the mantelpiece.
Forever stuck in clandestine stares
when words got stuck on mellow throats
and walls caved in, screaming speak now or
be forever exposed in every silly dream.

Perhaps the call was coming from inside the house
and let's say I answered,
since in every hypothesis I do.
But oblivion, for me, is supernatural
and tonight, starlets take the leading roles.

Ego

The corners were swept.
I checked, twice.
I licked the tiles and saw
how my bruised knees shined.
"It's nothing fancy" I said
while pouring you the bourbon.
"For you for you," I repeated
like a doll with lashes but no brain,
and you sat there all lovable.
Every sip dimmed your eyes.
I wish I had just sat down next to you
but I was busy portraying perfection.
For me, for me, it was always me.

Mary-Jane

Mary-Jane,
The apple of my eye, the sole of my shoe.
Are you an object or a subject if I burn for you?
Your iris garden, philosopher's pall…
You're a mutilated dream, like summer forced to fall.
Mary-Jane Mary-Jane
Where are you at?
You're a goose-feathered noose
I'm too soft to combat.

Shape Shifting

There's a loud knocking sound
outside the wooden door.
Some nights the shadows
of children run through the yard.
But no children live this far away.
I wake up every night, with an uneasy
feeling that someone is sitting on the bed.
I get up, search the lonely house.
The clock is frozen, once again
someone is giggling in the hallway.

As I approach the front door
I see light coming from under it.
There is no bulb in the lamp on the porch.
I lean against the door, hear the whispers.
There's a soft breeze that hovers in the air
"if only your dreams were truer than me."

Years went by, I left the house.
Whatever lived there with me,
had a beak like a blackbird.

The Flower That Bees Prefer

Behind Dolores, there's a glare in the sky.
Behind her, the midday turns into golden flames.
She stands with a paper cup and a paper plate,
and a paper plane in flames moves past her house.

Her cup rim is sucked wet, teeth marks of terror.
The juvenile mouth does whatever it can
not to narrate the burning sky.
The lawn is fresh-cut, and callow soot lingers.

Behind Dolores, there's a shadow upon her.
She knows that some days she's but a cloud.
A shadow keeps towering over the cerebral cortex.
Alto cumulus keeps setting on fire.

Extraterrestrial Affairs

This is what I remember,
a child leaning against a wall.
Cold crystal glass on her ear,
a dazzle of an oval-shaped gemstone,
lips tense with acute focus.
Eyes staring into the endless unknown.

She stood like this for hours
hearing stories of people
living behind the wall.
How could we tell her,
the next-door apartment
had always been empty.

The Blue Hour

The dream found its tamer–death,
Yet each night I tried to save you.
Your opal heart, my shapeless dread,
The entire summer just stood askew.

I carried you to your childbed,
Sang your song in mournful blue.
You slept until an arrowhead
Pierced our hope and found its view.

This Cycle Is Rounder Than The Moon

i. the cherry-scented morning arrives.
I see a human face approaching.
my pen and paper narrate each
minute. something is lost.

ii. my skin is a costume, and this
party never begins. I am the one
standing behind the story. your
prism of light feels electrifying.

iii. I give you a name after another.
try them out and click on a
Tiffany lamp. there's a yellow
couch that fits us two. you have
our beginning, but not my end.

iv. white walls drip color. bag of
cherries almost emptied. you're
my *deus ex machina*.
in denial of narration.

The Loud One Is Mine

Time opens up space, ready
to be altered as we like it.
I blink an eye and an entire hour
drops out of the clock face.
I catch minutes with an open mouth,
snowflakes summoned, saved
to meet me later, when time is yet
self-centered, needing attention.
I show the hidden minutes,
let me enjoy this a little longer…
I stood in the dark, I stood in all the silence.
I caressed you as you cried.

I hear them around, covering
all the eggshell white walls.
All the endless midnight calls.
There it is, the ticking, ticking
footsteps of death and ending.
I savored the minutes inside my flesh.
This is where I want to use them.
Don't cry now time, the sky is changing.
I need to see all of it, I am changing.
I need to feel all of it, hearts are like time
tick tick tick, the loud one is mine.

The Essence of Epione

Her hands read her fortune and mine.
Like a healer the touch is always invisible,
hidden sparks burst out of palms
and violets heavenly bloom.

She lives a life in the footnotes.
Calls herself an afterthought of sin,
but she is circumpolar,
a prayer of the blue moon.

Earthshine

I wish to be the sky filled with poetic clouds.
Strong enough to keep you from thunder, obligations.
Soft enough to let sunlight through, down Jacob's ladder.
Brobdingnagian, filled with rain, eager to quench your thirst.
To be an illusion if truth is unbearable.

I wish to be the sky filled with stories.
Cloud walker, effortlessly flowing quietude.
To reflect before drowning you in light.
Pouring down only in silence, unnoticed, at night.
So the dawns you wake up to would be evergreen.

I wish to be the sky filled with mysteries.
Carry an entire universe on my lap.
To be *eternal* yet never figured out.
I find you looking *to* the stars, for answers
when all of my constellations ask *you* to

look within yourself.

Zubenelgenubi

She swims under the September moon.
A silent wave flushes over her face.
I see soft lips forming bubbles under water,
sculpting a word: Zubenelgenubi.
"What nonsense," whisper all
the silver finned fish in the dark.

I float in black water with a grin on my face.
I know where to find it, what it means:
alpha librae with her tender silhouette.
A double star shining as vivid as ever.
I think we were neighbors.

Midnight talks, meteor showers:
a language essential for children
from a galaxy where time is hidden.
Hands draw circles on the blurred surface,
cool air embraces the autumn heatwave with full force.

"What are you two looking for, here, at night?"
ask the fish, creatures of yet another reality.
"Ourselves," we answer in a cosmic rhythm.

In Ink-Stained Letters, The Poet Has The Very Last Word

May I start my letter in dishabille, with my ink-sunken soul,
write open-ended questions about how you came to be.
Whether you played hide and seek in pastorals
with imaginary friends.
Whether you had shoes too big
as you traveled under the pink moon,
across moorland, fought dragons with a wood stick and sang
to the alligators in moats, carps in moss-eaten ponds,
saved mandarin ducks, fed them a tooth-peeled tangerine.

I pour a bottle of ink to wonder
whether you ran races with lemmings.
Slid along the riverbank holding fantasies on top of your hair.
Wore friendship bracelets on a blueberry-stained wrist,
wore a dress too long.
Whether you got your heart broken.
Stared out of spring pollen windows.
Whether you knew that life would be lived inside.
That they would lock your fairy-dream out.

Pareidolia

I wonder why I yearn so much,
under the drops of silver gloom.
To find someone, who would be such
to see a face on the moon.

With tender lips I asked around
what gentle eyes of others kiss.
Not any answer could astound
my gaze, which could never miss

the melancholy sense of night
As moon enchants the sky.
Like lovers staying out of sight
unable to grasp the why.

The eyes that shine the silver song
are eyes to which I solely long.

I Lean Out of a Dream

I lean out of a dream.
Head sticking out of a window
I see her,
in the blue hour of dawn.
I cannot comprehend how she would be here.
There is no path, no car in sight.
She has long legs, but it's a long way
through the blue dreamland.
Stars have their songs, of course,
and even the smallest one could travel
across the vastness of one mind.
This is making me nervous.
She keeps picking buttercups,
how could she not?
There's no way I'd allow myself to wake up now,
wherever we are,
this is simple,
this is good.

Andromeda

Mirrors are actually just openings
to Andromeda where I think worms
eat birds and birds breath under water.
I know people might look like us, they
come to the mirror as we do and stare at us.
When we hide the whites of our eyes, they
smile and move their limbs unexpecting
we would notice, they form round mouths,
blow cream dust and yell: *troglodyte!*

Artificial intelligence cradles us to the night
but we know, behind the wall there is a mirror
and the smiling smoke stays there waiting
for us to promise our bodies, our damaged
goods, it gets cold and under green flames
come the light, they stand in our bedroom nooks
in silence while we hide the whites of our eyes.
If we were to open them, we would admit
the mirror shows *us*, even when we sleep.
The reflections are coming, winds of
Andromeda.

Bird of Paradise

I'm devouring fruit like a bird of paradise.
I lift my face from empty fig shells.
Warm tongue. Wiping lips with bare hands.

Some feathered beings make us
iridescent, they see something
familiar and then wildly oscillate.

I have danced my dance through
a wild forest of cherry blossoms,
through riverbends and a paradox.

Juice of pears and peaches run down
my neck and ferns under fever play
Rachmaninov Piano Concerto No. 2.

The air around us is
adagio sostenuto,
slow and sustained.

Play Pretend

Let's pretend I haven't already sprinkled you all over me.
That this is the first time your presence is touching my tongue.
The first time I crawled through the fourth wall, to ask:

How am I making you feel?

Let's pretend you haven't timidly touched your neck before,
fingers coyly biding their time, suspended midair,
before going for my   figure
that this is the first time my words bend your spine.
Like you bend the spine of the book you're now reading.

One With The Clouds

I am one with clouds,
underneath me, towns bathe blessed.
My cries melt the hunger you once knew.
Here, phraseless volcanic sounds.

The bitter hour of the blue,
your haunting grace,
I come so close the air cracks:
massive waves of misplaced heat.

And when the sun meets the west,
the season of solemn death,
I speak of you in each electric socket,
this thunder has finally found its end.

Didi Aphra & Jonna Leine

And If You Look At Me, Do It Tenderly

Mono no aware-
A sensitivity to ephemera.

I am awakened to the early light of June,
and walking past the garden, I drink my coffee outside.
I take yesterday's pound cake from a brown paper bag,
eat one piece, throw the rest to the geese.

Where air draws a kiss on earth,
gray mist arises softly without a sound.
The day has begun again
and I am still   here

Bluebells in June

Carolina,
Do you remember how we lingered?
The endeavors for our saintly halos?
They told the story wrong.
There was you and me, and

Anteros told us we're too beautiful to look at.
I wonder how their hearts are now.

Carolina,
Was it a fig you gave me?
Or an apple? Or a supple taste of
a summer-born beast?
The gardens were gray, and they seemed *so* merry.

I stand in the evening light now
within me all of these endings.

Carolina,
I own a blue cup full of stars.
I wash it in soap water and then
touch my body as if it were yours.
Carolina, you're someone I could've missed.

Solace

How is our grief to be consoled
when touch is loaded,
within and around is a nebulous thunder.

Perhaps to look then is to comfort,
gaze as to embrace, tears forehead kisses
out of touch, a wonder to behold.

There is peculiar solace when rooms go still
looking away becomes an unbearable must
and the bond between two goes beyond eyes.

Hypothetically Speaking

It builds a loop.
I wake up serenading birds,
a wren fast asleep in the cotton-clouded nest.

The sky gives me vertigo.
Up beyond the treetop new worlds are unfolding.
It was a dream where I last met you.

All that was real is singing me asleep,
the small bird and its all-knowing eyes.
How can you know me before it begins?

I am a feathered cloud fast asleep.
Nothing has made sense for a while now.
Oh, how I am happy to be sad again.

Soul Contracts

Some nights after meditation,
I ask the cosmic blues whether I could–
instead of entering my own dream–
use my night invading yours.
"How dare you?!" I hear your voice.
The smallest star opens an eye.

The first night I floated in the dark.
I knew nothing, I knew everything,
an infant reminder of a complete mind.
The second night I saw a dim light.
A god, a god, a god,
scars healed.

Last night, an empty house.
On a windowsill, a candle was lit.
Where was I? Between two white crests
cascaded a purple shadow of all that is known.
And tonight, when I close my eyes,
will you be home?

Voyage of Galatea

Drop the mask before a sea of stars;
she's gazing again at distant waters.
Moon glades on dark velvet canvas,
she dives in through the tears of the ocean
where plankton glows amongst the beasts.

She swims in underwater galaxies,
stars tingle in serene eyes.
She is an asterisk of midnight,
wind blowing silver on quiet floating piers
where futures are made up, and forgotten.

Crush

I am a tin man, and so are you,
grown up in rain, left to search for a heart.

if you find your heart within another misfit,
you probably own theirs, so don't crush it

My tin foliage, rusty and awkward
unable to embrace with broken arms.

it's a broken system, where we are rushed
and yet time never catches our hearts

I encounter hearts made of silk and sawdust
placebo-love to create my own ointments.

the machine swallows each of us
crushing the life out, the pulsating organ

To stay whole in the world of humbugs,
where artificial gardens grow plastic apples,

I trust my heart to beat inside of you
use it fiercely, as only tin men do.

Unrepeatable Liaisons

I thought, in memory we'd become revived,
but I hold the night empty on my lap.
I have two hands but nowhere to place them,
a once wild and heated head
but no image to play with.

Remember my plain pleasure
when all I could imagine was starlike and real,
to laugh was the second-best verb
and present, all hours of one life.

The Stage of Nyx and the Paradise Dust

I am the night with wings,
apple-flavored skin bowing to the coiling strikes of thunder.
I run fast through the garden,
eye to eye with damp butterfly powder.
High peaks call me to be consumed by a tale, a star, the wind.
My light-filled ideals now wine-colored streams.
You ask about my favorite bird,
as if you haven't seen me soar.

Mornings pass me red-haired,
blue nostalgia smile, you have risen.
The universe seems to breathe through you.
You write about me in your journal,
cut my picture into pieces and burn it.
All I ever gave you was my innocence
under a strange new fig tree.

I pray you twice,
first for the "love me"
then for the show
            to end.
An art deco mind,
emptied edition.
Red clouds of roses.

Scarlet Eyes

Though life is only a part-time lover
and every aspect of it arbitrary,
I have to wonder why we would cover
our eyes, turn magic into ordinary.

A stream of people is passing you by,
and now you're held by an inquiring gaze.
The sounds, scents, a receding lullaby,
broken outlines of bodies, no sense of place.

So, you look into the cosmic unknown
and for some reason you are no longer lost.
But you break it like an ill-starred wishbone,
as if the look would have a dangerous cost.

Perhaps to hide the most scarlet eyes
we escape and pay the highest price.

Dissonance

There is the forest with ripe
cowberries, almost frosty.
Creeping light pushes through the twigs.
Spruces spit resin into my hair,
slower the rhythm of my steps.
I see your back furthering.
It's going to be dark soon.
Juniper eyes vacillate,
vanish with the season.

The dissonance comes in waves,
rushes scents of purple heathers,
admiration and solitude.
How strongly can words guide us
when forest blues bury them?
Should I turn back? Head home?
It's going to be cold soon.
Maybe you were an odd folk song,
never truly here, sighs from the past.
I press my temple against the pine.
I am true; in the dark, I am temporary.

Shadow Play

Ginger drink resting on a burnt thigh.
Red sun crawling behind the treetops.
"Show me the film," I whisper.
Silhouettes of pine trees reflected
on clouds stretched to the very sky.
Shadow puppetry presents stories
from Hades, dressed as dreams.
Lost member of altocumulus invades
the privacy I paid for, I ached for.
Muffled lines of devotion as the sun
eases its heat diving in the cold, simple sea.
Empty cocktail glass on the table,
deserted apartment, nightingale,
gentle breeze over wooden floor,
their shadows leaving ever-reaching stains on walls.

Didi Aphra & Jonna Leine

Pothos Carves Its Way Through My Walls

I touch people like ghosts do
as a figure in dreams
as a passing scent
as a vivid memory.

I never really use my limbs
the space between us grows a pothos vine
it is undulating with tension
never sober enough.

I never really become flesh
you sense my lips behind your neck
my fingertips reaching for yours
my feet pointing at you, always.

I touch people like ghosts do
as a figure in dreams
as a passing scent
as a fading memory.

Waldosia

I stay home a lot.
When I am out, every neck is yours.
Every shoulder, lock of hair.
Songs on the radio, each poem
on the melancholic postcards.
Oh, how tiring it is,
to be perpetually
met with only your shadow,
and never your light.

I Thought The End Would Be Eruptive

but what if every life
is the first
and the last
and through temporality
our amethyst brains
grow so fond of each other
we imagine a shared past
alternative endings
so that it never ends
but is an endless list of closing credits
of all that made us find this one string

if nothing is real
except this second, and this
and this
let me fill one more
with you

You, Calliope

Does the moon mirror my intentions,
place them into your nights?
I lie down on the cold, star-freckled tide,
you bathe in the silver river of magpies.
In the reflection of the moon aglitter in the water pools,
it sparks a definition, some kind of destination.
A moth flies, tender with a note,
sent my way, by Calliope:
under your soft, sculptured belly
the fluttering flight inside; is me.

All My Warmest Embraces Have Been Held Without Hands

The summer is hidden under a thin film of haze.
I watch memories become soft, like penumbras.
There are no faces anymore, no golden hours.
Light cuts through the lace curtain, drawing your
silhouette onto my sleeping skin.
I promise you, I know, still, all that
I knew back then. I wrote it down.

Did you know that

they had been asking, behind our backs
why I looked at you like a drowning one would look at land.
The answer is rather sweet, and innocent:
I had never known earth before.
The amber-covered ammonites on shore,
the forest green treetops with songbirds,
the blanket of galactic rush.

It felt safe to be seen.
To be embraced, without a single touch.

Notes

Fallen Fruit was first published with permission in the Dionysian Public Library's *Propagate: Fruits from the Garden* in 2024.

I'd like to give proper credit to Anne Carson's *If Not, Winter,* Allen Ginsberg's *Howl,* and Leigh Bardugo's *Ninth House* series, which are works I've directly quoted or referenced.

Didi

The poem title: *The Flower That Bees Prefer* is a reference to Emily Dickinson's poem title *There is a flower that bees prefer.*

Jonna

About the Poets

When Didi Aphra is not daydreaming or frolicking in the woods, she is concocting wondrous word potions in her lair. Didi has previously been published in COSY MAG and the Dionysian Public Library. Her work primarily explores mythology, belonging, and sexuality. Didi is currently working on a short story inspired by the ancient cults of Aphrodite. *Tender Philosophia* is her debut poetry book. Read more of her work on didiaphra.substack.com and find her on Instagram @didi.aphra.

Under the night sky, that is where to find Jonna Leine. Her hours are filled to the brim with marveling about existence and immersing herself in literary wonders. Jonna is a PhD candidate in comparative literature at the University of Turku. In her research and her writing, she explores the questions of identity, belonging, and the essence of a good life. She prefers to be surrounded by beautiful dreamscapes and has a degree in interior design from the Helsinki Design School. She also works as a songwriter in Finland and has received an honorary mention in a writing contest organized by the Oulu Writers Association and The Summer University of Northern Ostrobothnia. *Tender Philosophia* is her debut poetry book. Read more of her work on jonnaleine.substack.com and find her on Instagram @jonnaleine.

www.ingramcontent.com/pod-product-compliance
Lightning Source LLC
Chambersburg PA
CBHW020529160726
47992CB00005BA/2303